This book belongs to:

Thank you for picking up this coloring book! Here, you'll find a collection of beautiful illustrations just waiting for your artistic touch. Whether you're looking for a moment of peace or a burst of creative energy, we hope this book provides you with endless hours of enjoyment. Happy coloring!

LIA CARVALHO

TEST COLOR PAGE